Heinrich Brugsch

Verzeichnis der Hyroglyphen mit Lautwert in der gewöhnlichen und in der geheimen Schrift

Heinrich Brugsch

Verzeichnis der Hyroglyphen mit Lautwert in der gewöhnlichen und in der geheimen Schrift

ISBN/EAN: 9783743451643

Hergestellt in Europa, USA, Kanada, Australien, Japan

Cover: Foto ©Paul-Georg Meister /pixelio.de

Manufactured and distributed by brebook publishing software (www.brebook.com)

Heinrich Brugsch

Verzeichnis der Hyroglyphen mit Lautwert in der gewöhnlichen und in der geheimen Schrift

VERZEICHNISS

DER HIEROGLYPHEN MIT LAUTWERTH

IN DER GEWÖHNLICHEN UND IN DER GEHEIMEN SCHRIFT

SOWIE

DER ALLGEMEINEN DEUTZEICHEN

IN DEM SCHRIFTSYSTEM DER ALTEN ÄGYPTER

MIT HINWEIS AUF SEIN HIEROGLYPHISCHES WÖRTERBUCH ZUSAMMENGESTELLT

VON

HEINRICH BRUGSCH

LEIPZIG

J. C. HINRICHS'SCHE BUCHHANDLUNG

1872

Uebersicht der Hieroglyphen mit phonetischem Werthe.

Die folgende Uebersicht gewährt ein möglichst vollständiges Verzeichniss der hieroglyphischen Charactere, welche alphabetischen oder syllabischen Werth haben, mit Einschluss der Polyphonen. Wir haben Sorge getragen, die phonetischen Werthe beizufügen, welche die geheime oder änigmatische Schrift diesen Zeichen beilegt. Die fragliche Schrift, deren Spuren wir bis ins Zeitalter der Ramessiden zurückverfolgen können und welche sich unter den Ptolemäern zum System entwickelt, beruht auf dem akrophonischen Principe, welches einem beliebigen Zeichen den Laut des Anfangsbuchstabens seines syllabischen Werthes oder des Wortes oder mehrerer Wörter, welche ihm in der gesprochenen Sprache entsprechen, beilegt. So wird z. B. das Silbenzeichen  *nu* in dieser Schrift zu dem einfachen Consonanten *n* und das Bild des Widder  bezeichnet bald den Consonanten  *b*, bald den Consonanten  *s*, weil der Widder in der ägyptischen Sprache bald durch das Wort  *ba*, bald durch das Wort  *ser* bezeichnet wird. Es kann dies Schriftsystem mithin nicht unpassend das der Akrophonie heissen.

Da der Laut der Sprache im Laufe der Jahrhunderte manchen Wechseln und Veränderungen sowohl consonantischer als vokalischer Natur unterlegen ist, so ist es gekommen, dass die An- und Auslaute der Silbenzeichen in verschiedenen Epochen öfter verschieden sind und dass die jüngere Aussprache der antiken nicht mehr entspricht. So wurden z. B. , ,  ursprünglich  *år*,  *åp*,  *āb*, später aber  *īri*,  *up*,  *ub*, gleichwie im Koptischen ⲓⲣⲓ, ⲱⲡ und ⲟⲩⲏⲃ gesprochen.

Solche Veränderungen betreffen hauptsächlich die folgenden Buchstaben:

	*å*	wird	ersetzt	durch	 *a*,  *ā*,  *ū*,  *u*,  *ī*.
	*ā*	»	»	»	 *å*,  *ū*,  *u*.
	*b*	»	»	»	 *p*,  *m*,  *ū*
	*f*	»	»	»	 *ū*,  *u*.
	n	»	»	»	 *r*,  *l*.

 s wird ersetzt durch  *š*.

 *ḥ* » » »  *χ*.

 *χ* » » »  *ś*.

 t » » »  *t*,  *t*,  *t*.

 *k* » » »  *q*,  *g*.

Andere Veränderungen entstehen durch die Liquidierung und Abwerfung des Consonanten  *r*, besonders des auslautenden; z. B.  *áner* und  *án*,  *bener* und  *ben*,  =  *χeper* und  *χep*,  =  *kers* und  *kes*, und dergleichen mehr. Auch die Metathesis findet sich häufig, z. B.  = 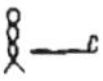 *ḥā* und 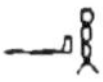 *āḥ*,  =  *tá* und  *át*,  =  *ān* und  *nā*,  = 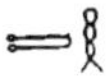 *teḥ* und  *ḥet*,  =  *seš* und  *šes*, u. s. w.

In der folgenden Uebersicht bezeichnet

A, dass der phonetische Werth, dem der Buchstabe beigefügt ist, den Texten des alten Reiches angehört;

B, dass der phonetische Werth nur der Schrift der späten Epoche, der Akrophonie, eigen ist;

* dass der Character mit diesem phonetischen Werthe sich in unserm Wörterbuche, dessen Seitenzahl wir den übrigen Zeichen beigefügt haben, nicht befindet.

I. Figuren von Männern.

No.	Zeichen	Werth	Wb. Pag.
1		*àn*	81
2		*ḥa̧*	886
3		*ān*	191
		ā B.	
4		*ur*	332
5	,	*ser*	1261
		s B.	
		ā B.	
6		*àti*	149
7	,	*sa*	1150
		s	
8	, B.	*fa*	534
		ket	
		f B.	
9		*nini*	743
10		*àau*	32
		ten	1550
11		*set*	1336
12		*ṭu* B.	1609
		ṭ B.	
13		*āχ*	213
14		*kers*, *kes*	1475
15		*ḥeter*	1010
16		*χeχet**	
17		*ka*	1435
		k B.	
		ḥāā	935
		ḥ B.	
18		*n* B.	
19	, B.	*neχt*	802

No.	Zeichen	Werth	Wb. Pag.
20		*ṭua̧*	1621
21		*àb*	35
22		*ḳoṭ*	1477
23		*χus*	1063
24		*ba*	
25	,	*seher*	9[illegible]3
26		*āb**	
27		*tut*	1532
28		*kers*	1470
29		*à*	gr.10.
30		*à*	gr.92.
31		*àm*	78
32		*àr*	94
33		*sa*	1158
		s	
34		cf. No. 7	
35		cf. No. 8	
36		*ḥeḥ*	989
		ḥ B.	
37		*ḥeḥ*	989
		ḥ B.	
		nefer	757
38		*šep*	1381
39		*àmen*	cf. 71
40		*tḥuti**	
		à B.	
41		*usàr**	
		s B.	

N⁰.	Zeichen	Werth	Wb. Pag.
42		*un* **B.**	253
43		*šu*	1151
		s **B.**	
44		*ten*	1549
45		*àmen*	71
46		*set*	1354
47		*āb*	171
		*ub**	
48		*χer*	1116
49		*sen*	1243
50		*meḥ*	689
51		*neb*	745
52		*neb*	747
53		*nem*	1101
54		*s*	1151
		nen **B.**	
		n **B.**	
		χen **B.**	
		χ **B.**	800
		šerà **B.**	1404
		ā **B.**	

II. Figuren von Frauen.

N⁰.	Zeichen	Werth	Wb. Pag.
55		*ḳeb*	1509
56		*bok*	428
57		*bok**	
58		*beχ*	cf. 412
		mes	696
		pāpā	413
59		*net**	
		n **B.**	

N⁰.	Zeichen	Werth	Wb. Pag.
60		*šeta** **B.**	
61		*maā*	
		m **B.**	
62		*tūa* **B.**	1621

III. Glieder des menschlichen Körpers.

N⁰.	Zeichen	Werth	Wb. Pag.
63		*tep*	1535
		āp	1539
		*ḥer**	
64		*ḥer*	977
65		*ànem*	90
		ḥā	931
		*her**	
66		*uta*	312
		bok	427
67		*àb**	
68		*àt*	136
		tà	1527
69		*àn*	85
		nā	739
		ān	193
70		*ma**	
71		*àn*	193
		ān	193
72		*àr*	97
		īri **B.**	
		ī **B.**	
		men **B.**	
		mer	675

No.	Zeichen	Werth		Wb. Pag.
73		*ȧr*		100
74		*ȧr*		100
75		*mer*		675
76		*ṭebḥ*		1633
77		*ṭebḥ*		1633
78		*ȧm*		63
		ṡem		1235
79		*r*		838
80	,	*neb*		748
81		*beḥ*	*A.*	1632
		ḥu		938
		ḥ	*B.*	
82		*sepeṭ*		1205
83		*ūr*		211
84	,	*χa̤bes*		1031
85		*sa**	*B.*	
86		, *ka*		1433
		, *k*	*B.*	
87	,	*χen**		
88	, ,	*nen*		776
		n	*B.*	
89		*ā*		
		toṭ		1665
90		*sop**		
		meḥ		692
91		*ni̥ni̥*		743
92		*mo*		596
93		*mo*		596
		m		596

No.	Zeichen	Werth		Wb. Pag.
		ḥonk		970
94		*mok*		617
95		*neχṭ*		802
		*n**	*B.*	
96		*ṭu*		1609
		*ṭ**	*B.*	
97		*ṭeser*		1682
		ṭeser		1682
98	,	*χu*		1061
99		*ḥi*		914
100		*ser*		1259
101		*uṭen*		307
102		*χen*		1104
103		*ȧm*		64
104		*seṭ*	*B.*	
105		*ṭ*		1604
106	,	*kep*		1491
107		*šep*		1376
108		*šep*		1376
109		*šep*		1376
110		*ḥen*		965
111		*īā*		231
112		*tep*	*A.*	
		*ṭeb**		
		ṭebā		1678
113		*maā**		574
114		*ṭa**		1703
115		*ān*		cf. 201
116		*ka*		1435
		beḥ		410

No.	Zeichen	Werth	Wb. Pag.
		met	720
		mo	721
		ta	cf. 1704
		t B.	
		*per**	
117		*men*	636
118		*ḥen*	1726
119		*sem*	1222
120		*tu**	
		t B.	
121		*àī*	233
122		*seb*	1185
123		*sem*	1222
124		*śem*	1386
125		*nen*	773
		n B.	
		àn	82
126		*śes*	1407
127		*tet*	1537
		t B.	
128		*pet*	518
		rot	877
		uār	244
		men	639
129		*toh*	1562
130		*b*	
131		*ḳer*	1515
132		*āā*	542
		àā	542
		fuā	542

No.	Zeichen	Werth	Wb. Pag.
		às	121
133		*sem*	1217
134		*śāṭ*	1364
135		*seper*	1202
136		*àuf*	59
		f	
137		*ḥū*	934

IV. Vierfüssler.

No.	Zeichen	Werth	Wb. Pag.
138		*l*	883
		ār	205
		àr	205
		śenā	1400
139		*ser* B.	1261
140		*ma*	505
		ma B.	gr. 76
		śenā	1400
141		*neb*	745
142		*χeb*	1031
		tep	1635
		teb	1629
143		*ser*	1259
144		*āb*	168
145		*sa*	1151
146		*sep*	1198
		sāb	1163
		śa	1422
		*ān** B.	
		*ī** B.	
147		*set*	1331

No.	Zeichen	Werth	Wb. Pag.
148		*set* A.	
149		*sešta*	1316
150		*ān*	163
		à B.	
		sa	1154
		*ṭeṭ** B.	
		*ṭe** B.	
151		*ȧn* B.	
152		*kenṭ*	1463
153		*nefer* B.	757
154		*set*	
155		*nefer* B.	757
156		*nefer* B.	757
		sem	1235
157		*ka*	1435
		k B.	
158		*neb* B.	745
159		*beχ* B.	412
160		*nāš* B.	741
161		*ḥes*	993
162		*fu*	538
		àā	542
		āā	542
163		*àb*	35
164		*ba*	370
		b B.	
		ser	1259
		s B.	
165		*sūą*	1163

No.	Zeichen	Werth	Wb. Pag.
166		*āu*	1719
		ā B.	
		*ār** B.	
		š B.	
167		*sāḥ*	1170
168		*šes**	
		š B.	
169		*šes* B.	
170		*χeχ** B.	
171		*ma* B.	
172		*χeft* (*mat?*) B.	

V. Glieder von Vierfüsslern.

No.	Zeichen	Werth	Wb. Pag.
173		*peḥ*	496
174		*ḥā*	931
175		*ḥā* B.	931
176		*peteḥ*	527
177		*neb** B.	
178		*at*	20
		ta	20
179		*sesennu** B.	
180		*hau* B.	906
181		*teḥ*	1664
		*ḥet**	
182		*šes*	1311
		seš	1308
183		*ṭenṭen*	1648
184		*ken*	1728
185		*šef*	1383

Nº.	Zeichen	Werth		Wb. Pag.
186		*set*		1331
187		*set*	A.	1331
188		*pau**	B.	
189		*us*		276
		*ḥā**	B.	
190		*bȧ*		372
191		id.	B.	
192		*r*	B.	
193		*χen*		1094
194		*fet*		
		χent		1108
		sen		
		*tep**	A.	
195		*sem*		1344
		setem		1344
		ṭen		1641
		ȧṭ		153
		*seṭ**		
196		*ȧp*		52
		up	B.	
197		*ȧau*		32
198		*āb*		167
		*ub**	B.	
199		*ȧp*		58
		*up**	B.	
200		*χnem*	B.	1097
201		*ṭem*		1640
202		*ām*		185
		ā	B.	

Nº.	Zeichen	Werth		Wb. Pag.
203		*neḥ*		491
204		*ḥekạ*		1001
205		*āb*		175
206		*nem**	A.	-
207		*nem* (?)		769
208		*kep*		1491
		kep		1491
209		*sek*		1319
210		*ȧs*		121
211		*seṭ*		1349

VI. Vögel.

Nº.	Zeichen	Werth		Wb. Pag.
212		*ḥor*		982
		*neter**	B.	
		bȧk		
		*p**	B.	
213		*neb**		
214		*ba*		370
		b	B.	
215		*ba**	B.	
		b	B.	
216		*χu*		114
		χ	B.	
217		*āk*		221
218		*uš*		284
219		*šerȧ*		1404
220		*ur*		332
221		*ba*		370
		b	B.	
222		*bek*		424

No.	Zeichen	Werth	Wb. Pag.
223		*mert*	731
		met	731
		m	596
		ner	786
		*keṭ** B.	
224		*menχ* B.	660
225		*teχ*	1664
		teḥ	1664
226		*sa*	1151
		s B.	
		r B.	
		u B.	
		men	656
		ḥep	951
227		*mer*	730
		mer	730
228		*àm*	559
		m	
229		*neḥ*	792
		n B.	
230		*neḥ*	792
		n B.	
231		*kem*	1451
		ḳam A.	1451
232		*ṭeśer*	1659
		ṭeś	1659
233		*ṭef*	1680
234		*ti*	gr. 5
235		*seḥ*	1277

No.	Zeichen	Werth	Wb. Pag.
236		*a*	1
237		*u*	238
238		*bāḥ*	381
239		*ḥem*	958
240		*set*	1353
241		*ṭeb*	1629
242		*pa*	448
		p B.	
243		*sep** A.	
		ḥenā B.	1726
244		*χen*	1089
245		*kema*	1452
		ten	1549
246		*χu* B.	1062
247		*reχ*	869
248		*mok* B.	617
249		*ṭa*	1702
250		*men*	667
		set	73
251		*sont*	1256

VII. Glieder von Vögeln.

No.	Zeichen	Werth	Wb. Pag.
252		*χu* B.	114
253		*ner*	785
254		*ṭeṭ*	1686
		ṭ	1673
255		*pek*	514
256		*meḥ* B.	692
		seś	1310

No.	Zeichen	Werth		Wb. Pag.
257		ȧmaχ	B.	75
258		meḥ		690
259		remen		853
		nen		780
260		ṡa*		
261		muā		574
		m	B.	
		ṡu		1365
		ṡ	B.	
		keb		1444
262		sa		1151
		s	B.	
263	,	ān		202
	VIII. Fische.			
264		ȧn		96
		s	B.	
265		χa		1041
266		betu		439
267	.	sep		
268		bes		418
269		nār		741
270		ān		193
		ȧn		
271		neb		86
	IX. Amphibien und Reptile.			
272		sebek		1194
		sek		1193
		aṭ*		22
		n	B.	
273		mu	B.	633
274		āχ*		
		āṡ	B.	220
		ṭem		1639
275		ro, r	B.	841
276		ru*		
		r	B.	
		f	B.	
277		neb		745
		r	B.	
		k	B.	
278		ṭ		
279		meḥ		694
280		ṭet		1683
281		meṭ?		
282		ker	B.	1466
283		ken		1458
284	,	f		
285		per		449
286		āk		221
287		ȧter		143
288		sata	B.	
289		ḥek		1000
290		ḥefen		955
291		āf		185
		men		644
		seχet		1303
		χeb		1063
		ket		1477
292		χeper		1071
		χep		1071

N°.	Zeichen	Werth	Wb. Pag.
		ṭa B.	1522
		t B.	
293		*āp* B.	179
		ā B.	
294		*ḥotp* B.	1005
295		*serk*	1269
296		*kem*	1448

X. Bäume, Pflanzen, Blumen u. s. w.

N°.	Zeichen	Werth	Wb. Pag.
297		*àm*	63
		m B.	594
298		*àtf* B.	139
299		*χet*	1138
		χer B.	1116
		χ B.	1050
300		*un*	253
301		*ḥen*	961
		às	120
302		*neḥem* B.	796
		n B.	
303		*neχeb* B.	799
		n B.	
304		*ūaḥ*	342
305		*sek*	1323
306		*benr*	398
		ben	396
		mor	606
		m B.	
307		*notem*	834
		nem A.	
308		*ūat*	354

N°.	Zeichen	Werth	Wb. Pag.
309		*ṭqui* B.	
310		*χa*	1022
		χ B.	
311		*ḥen*	972
312		*ùr* B.	332
313		*χesef*	1134
314		*àtḥ*	27
		meḥ	690
		χeb	1063
315		*ḥa*	916
		ḥ B.	
316		*neχeb*	799
		n B.	
317	B.	*nen*	774
		n B.	765
318		*su*	1173
		s B.	
319		*riṣ*	871
320		*kemā*	1453
321		*rep*	855
		renp	861
		sep?	
322		*keṭ* B.	1478
323		*ter*	1553
324		*š*	
325		*sem*	1229
		s B.	
		seχet	1303
		u B.	

N°.	Zeichen	Werth	Wb. Pag.
326		*à*	
327		*ī*	
328		*mes*	695
329		*boti*	442
330	,	*ḥet*	1015
		ḥet B.	
331	,	*son*	1237
		s B.	
332		*χaī*	1022
333		*tà*	1527
334		*àp*	49
335		*r* B.	
336	, ,	*roṭ*	878
337		*ḥen*	963
338		*às*	119
339	,	*ter*	1556

XI. Himmelskörper.

N°.	Zeichen	Werth	Wb. Pag.
340		*pet*	452
		p B.	989
		ḥer	979
		χī	1058
		men B.	638
341	,	*teḥen*	1589
342		*ker*	1466
343	, ,	*rā*	848
		r B.	
344		*χu*	112
		χ B.	
345		*χu*	112
		χ B.	

N°.	Zeichen	Werth	Wb. Pag.
		àm	68
346		*ḥuṭ*	1015
347		*āp** B.	
		ā B.	
348		*ḥeḥ* B.	
349		*χā*	1052
		χ B.	
		š B.	
350	,	*àb*	45
		à B.	
351		*šep*	1379
352		*seb*	1182
		s B.	
		ṭūa	1621
		ṭ B.	
		χabs	

XII. Erde, Berge, Inseln, Steine.

N°.	Zeichen	Werth	Wb. Pag.
353	,	*ta*	1521
		t B.	
354		*ṭu*	1608
		men B.	638
		ā B.	
		ḥ B.	
355		*men*	667
356		*ḥ* B.	
357	,	*sep** A.	
		n B.	
358		*àa*	29
		ān	1338
		àn	
359	,	*àner*	90

No.	Zeichen	Werth		Wb. Pag.
		àn		90
		men	B.	655

XIII. Wasser, Flüssigkeiten, Becken.

No.	Zeichen	Werth		Wb. Pag.
360		mu		633
		m	B.	
361		n		
		mu	B.	633
362	,	χen		1095
		men	B.	
		à	B.	866
363	,	š		
364	,	n	B.	
365	,	mer		669
		m	B.	
366	,	hà		374
		ḥem		956
		peḥ		494
367		tef		1543
		pu	B.	464
		ru		
368		āb		171
		ub	B.	
369		āb		171
		ub	B.	

XIV. Städte, Gebäude, Zimmer, Theile des Hauses u. s. w.

No.	Zeichen	Werth		Wb. Pag.
370		nen		773
		nu		773
371		per		449
		p	B.	449
372		ḥet		1003
		ḥ	B.	
		χ	B.	
373		seḥ		1272
		ārk		1273
374		ḥeb		942
375		àft		60
376		ḥā		212
		āḥ		—
377		ànb *		cf. 89
378		useχ		279
379		neter		823
380		χem		1082
381	,	su		1153
		s	B.	
		ro	B.	
382	,	χet		746
		ār		205
		ā	B.	
383		neh		787
		ken		1461
384		sebeχ		1191
385	,	ā		158
386	s	ses		1305
		s		
387		m		
388		àn		83
		à	B.	
389		men		636
		teχen		1567

Nº.	Zeichen	Werth	Wb. Pag.
		ṭ B.	
390		*ṭeṭ*	1663
		ṭ B.	
		pseṭ	510
391		*åkep** B.	
392		*s*	1152
		ås B.	
		us B.	
		men	640
393		*us**	
		utes	309

XV. Waffen, schneidende Geräthe, Geisseln u. s. w.

Nº.	Zeichen	Werth	Wb. Pag.
394		*neter*	823
395		*ṭem*	1630
		ṭes	1380
		ṭes	1380
		n B.	
396		*moten* B.	625
397		*sem*	1222
398		*sem*	—
399		*nem*	763
400		... *ḥu* ... B.	1710
401		*sek*	1319
402		*tep*	1335
403		*āa*	158
		ā B.	
404		*uā*	241
405		*set*	
406		*sun*	1174

Nº.	Zeichen	Werth	Wb. Pag.
407		*set* B.	1335
408		*set*	1336
409		*peṭ*	519
410		*kens*	1497
		*χont**)	
411		*šemer*	1392
412		*χer*	1227
413		*keṭ*	1478 1484
		sat A.	
414		*ma*	561
415		*meḥ*	684
416		*šeṭ*	1413
417		*χu* B.	1061
		χ B.	
418		*χeb*	1063
419		*ṭem* B.	1640
420		*ṭebḥ* B.	

XVI. Scepter, Insignien u. s. w.

Nº.	Zeichen	Werth	Wb. Pag.
421		*ḥek*	924
422		*āu*	1719
423		*us*	348
424		*sem*	1226
425		*seχem*	1289
426		*χorp*	1129
427		*men*	667
		*set**	
428		*χu*	1061

No.	Zeichen	Werth	Wb. Pag.
429		*āb*	168
430		*seχmer*	1230

XVII. Stöcke, Keulen u. s. w.

No.	Zeichen	Werth	Wb. Pag.
431		*s*	
432		*àm* A.	63
433		*ām*	187
		ā B.	
		tā	1076
		*neh̨**	
		kem	1451
		k̨em A.	
		*ka**	
		*k̨a**	
434		*āb*	170
435		*seteb*	1352
436		*m* B.	
437		*χen*	1092
438		*nem* A.	767
439		*ut*	291
440		*āb*	1719
441		*tet*	1686
		t	
442		*t*	1673
443		*ta*	
444		*men*	636
445		*nem*	767

XVIII. Instrumente und Geräthschaften.

No.	Zeichen	Werth	Wb. Pag.
446		*tes*	1592
		res	871
447		*res*	871
448		*āb*	168
		ḳes	1473
		ḳen	1513
		bet	441
		mesen	699
449		*seh*	1275
450		*net*	827
		net B.	
		n B.	
451		*āb*	172
		ub B.	
		ām	189
452		*menχ*	660
453		*χa*	1042
		χ B.	
454		*sa*	1161
455		*sa*	1154
		s B.	
456		*sam*	1214
		s B.	
457		*nen*	777
		n B.	
458		*setp*	1341
		*ānp**	
459		*utā*	310

Nº.	Zeichen	Werth		Wb. Pag.
460		*i*		
461		*ḥen*		965
462		*mer*		669
		ma	*B.*	
		m	*B.*	
463		*heb*		895
		per		479
464		*seḥotp*	*B.*	1281
465		*nanu*	*B.*	

XIX. Musikalische Instrumente und Spiele.

Nº.	Zeichen	Werth		Wb. Pag.
466		*nefer*		757
467		*ḥes**	*B.*	
468		*seχem*		1292
469		*men*		636
470		*àb*		36
471		*maā*		574
		m	*B.*	
472		*sa*		1156
		s	*B.*	

XX. Kronen.

Nº.	Zeichen	Werth		Wb. Pag.
473		*nefer*	*B.*	757
		n	*B.*	
		ḥet		1016
474		*net*		821
		n	*B.*	
		teser		1659
475		*k*	*B.*	684
476		*meḥ*		684
477		*meḥ*		684
478		*ten**		
479		*šu*		1367
480		*seχet*		1303

XXI. Bänder, Binden, Knoten, Kleider.

Nº.	Zeichen	Werth		Wb. Pag.
481		*kes*		1475
		k, ḳ	*B.*	
		ser		1262
		s	*B.*	
		*šes**		
482		*menī*		648
483		*šen*		1393
484		*rot*		879
485		*šen*		1394
486		*ḥ*		
487		*menχ*		662
488		*ut*		246
		tet		1684
		ḥeseb		994
		ā	*B.*	
489		*u*		
490		*set*		1331
		set		1331
		às		118
		as		15
491		*set*		1331
492		*tem**	*B.*	
493		*ūq*		

No.	Zeichen	Werth	Wb. Pag.
494		*seḥ*	
		seχet	1303
495		*menȧ*	645
496		*an*	9
497		*sent*	1255
498		*ārk*	209
499		*mer*	668
500		*nes*	803
		ṭep	1634
		r *B.*	
501		*set*	1335
502		*āṭ*	227
503		*tes*	1593
504		*net*	
		n *B.*	
505		*kep*	1491
506		*s* *B.*	
507		*sa*	1154
		s *B.*	
508		*āper*	161
509		*ṭeb*	1624
		*ṭeb** *A.*	
510		*neb*	745
511		*χaker*	1048
512		*šen*	1394
513		*sāḥ*	1170
514		*ānχ*	197

XXII. Mathematische Figuren.

No.	Zeichen	Werth	Wb. Pag.
515		*χ*	
516		*neker*	814
517		*sep*	1196
518		*pāt* *A.*	
519		*pau*	457
520		*t*	
521		*χemt**	
522		*k, q*	
523		*ḥu*	938
		ḥ *B.*	
524		*sept*	1205
		sebṭ	1205
525		*ṭu*	1609
		ṭ *B.*	
		t *B.*	
526		*p*	
527		*ȧ*	
528		*i*	
529		*men* *B.*	638
530		*ḥep*	949
531		*uu*	238
		ur	332
		seš	1308
		su	1180
532		*h*	
533		*mer*	671
534		*rer*	863
535		*ten*	1585
536		*ṭeben*	1631
537		*ren*	860
538		*šu*	
539		*ṭenȧ*	1643
		peχ	511
		peš	511

N°.	Zeichen	Werth		Wb. Pag.
540		*ṭenà*		1644
541		*ḥer*		983
542		*āu*		112
		voir No. 358		
543		*sen*		1239
544		*ṭeṭ*		
545		*qen*		1463
		ṭaṭa		1701
546		*χem*		1291
		u	*B.*	
547		*men*	*B.*	636
548		*àp*		48
549		*uteb*		297
550		*uṭen*		305

XXIII. Gefässe, Flaschen, Körbe, Schalen u. s. w.

N°.	Zeichen	Werth		Wb. Pag.
551		*nu*		772
		nu̥n		772
		n	*B.*	
		men		654
		χu̥n		1094
552		*teχ*		1564
553		*nem*	*A.*	
		χnem		1097
554		*àb*		36
555		*fu*	*B.*	582
556		*nu̥n*		774
557		*ḥos*		989
558		*χont*		1108
559		*keb*		1441
560		*ḥon*		973
		ḥ	*B.*	
561		*ma*		566
562		*šeṭ*		1414
		šeṭ		1414
563		*āu*		158
		ā	*B.*	
		āb		169
		ḥon		977
		useχ		278
564		*ba*	*B.*	
		b	*B.*	
565		*ta*		1523
		t	*B.*	
566		*ta*		1523
		t	*B.*	
567		*seḥ* *		
568		*ta*		1523
569		*bes*		418
		b	*B.*	
570		*mer*	*B.*	675
571		*ḳa*		1728
		mesen		703
572		*ḥotep*		1005
573		*ḥen*		900
574		*àa*		138
		à	*B.*	
575		*ḳ*		
576		*nes*		801
		n	*B.*	

No.	Zeichen	Werth	Wb. Pag.
577		χer	
		χ B.	
578		kata	1503
579		k	
580		neb	744
		n B.	
581		ḥeb B.	942
582		ān	190
		nā	740

XXIV. Schiffe und ihre Theile.

No.	Zeichen	Werth	Wb. Pag.
583		χont	1110
		s B.	
584		χu B.	
585		àm	594
		m B.	
586		uā	1708
587		ḥep	949
		χer	1119
588		ḥem	957
589		nef	755
		t B.	

No.	Zeichen	Werth	Wb. Pag.
590		ḥā	927
		āḥ	927
		ḥ B.	
		āb A.	1168
591		nem	764
		met	628

XXV. Gerüste und Gestelle.

No.	Zeichen	Werth	Wb. Pag.
592		χont	1108
593		χep A.	
		kep	1376
594		fu	540
595		ḥer	982
		meten	625
596		tem	1545
597		àmaχ	75
598		seχt	1301
599		nem	764
600		àm	63
		m B.	

Uebersicht der gebräuchlichsten generellen Determinativa.

No.	Zeichen	determiniert	No.	Zeichen	determiniert
1		To speak, to name, to implore, to read.	20		Rest, inactivity, infirmity, to sit.
2		To worship, to greet.	21		God, goddess, eminent, sacred person.
3		To adore, to praise, to sing.	22		A God, Ancestor, sacred personage.
4		To return, to turn oneself.	23		Enemy, wickedness, crime.
5		Height, joy.	24		Soldier, troop, great number.
6	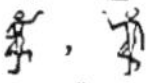	Sport, Exultation.	25		Sacred person. Ancestor.
7		Great, greatness.	26		To rest, to sit.
8		Age, parent, frailty.	27		Child, youth, revival.
9		To carry, to burden, to work.	28		To throw down, to greet, to salute, to worship, to kill, to overthrow, battle.
10		To beat, to strike, severe handling, or acting.			
11		To plough, to cultivate, to build on.	29		Slaughter, overthrow.
12		Enemy, Wickedness, hostility.	30		To die, deceased, to bury, to embalm.
13		To unite, to combine, connection.	31	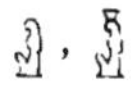	Goddess, woman, female name.
14	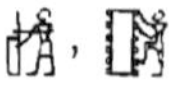	To build, to construct, to form.	32		Goddess, woman. female name.
15		Form, figure, portrait, type, to assemble, to unite, to set up, custom, mummy, burial.	33		Pregnancy, with child.
			34		Born, descent, race, birth.
16		Individual, person, denotes any office held by man.	35		To absorb, to nourish, to bring up.
17		Activity with the mouth. Idea, word, to declare.	36		Head, mind, genius, uppermost, pre-eminence, superiority.
18		To bear, to burden, to work.	37		Hair, skin, colour, grief, pain.
19		To worship, to hail, to invoke, to ask for, to read.	38		Eye, sun, moon, mouth, bud.

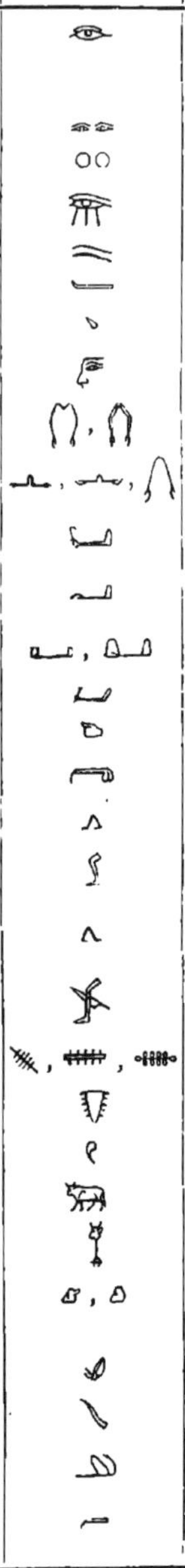

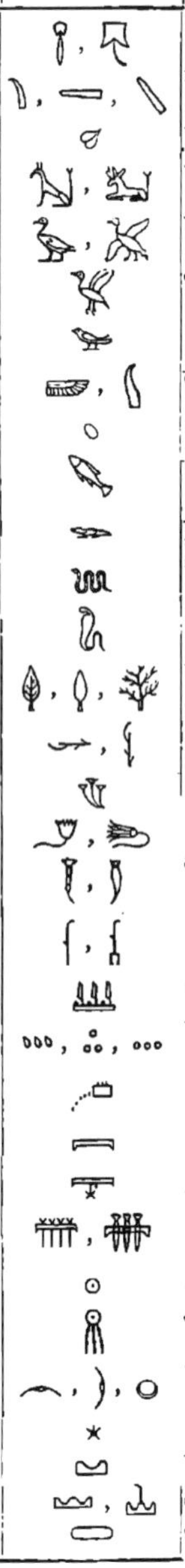

Nº.	Zeichen	determiniert
39		To see, perceive, to try, to mark, to watch, guards, to awake, to sleep, repose, to repose, to dream, to die.
40		"
41		"
42		To weep, tear, pain, affliction, sadness,
43		Eyebrows.
44		To taste, to eat, to speak.
45		To taste, to [illegible], to speak
46		To breathe, to enjoy, to feel, joy, desire.
47		Embrace, unite, agree,
48		To deny, to keep [illegible], to defend.
49		Severe handling, to beat, to take, to grasp.
50		Gentle handling, to assent, consent, arm. poor.
51		To present, to pour, to fill, to give
52		To write, to paint, to draw, picture.
53		To seize, to hold, to contain.
54		masculine, manly, to plow, ensue, to soil, before, from, with, since, in preference to.
55		To go, to step, to advance, to march.
56		To exceed, to measure with steps, leg, bone, foot, bottom, pedestal, base, way of life, instrument for measuring
57		To turn oneself, to return, to turn [illegible], backward, back.
58		To tread over, to join, to transgress, to trespass, to go over. [illegible] to avoid, surpass, excell, exceed
59		spine, backbone, back, ridge, rear, to cut off, to cut to pieces.
60		"
61		Flesh, parts of animals bodies.
62		Quadruped.
63		Throat, voice, channel, flute, gorge, to breathe, enjoy, to eat, victuals.
64		Nose, scent, rebuke, to breathe, enjoy, to feel, to snore, to bluster, comfort, desire, to block up.
65		To hear, obey, listen, ear, handle.
66		Horn, skin (hard) feelers (of insects) single horn, peak of a mount, to attack, weather resistance.
67		Behind, at the end, on the reserved side, strength, power, energy, virtue, force, to follow, succeed, obey.
68		Paw, claw, seize, pull away, strong, to rob.
69		Skin, coat, tunicle, quadruped.
70		Tail, train, end.
71		Testicle, stone.
72		Set, or Typhon, power, danger, misfortune.
73		Bird, to fly, to fly away, to blow.
74		To remain, to continue, to perish, to halt, pasture-ground.
75		Wickedness, spite
76		wing, harpsichord, to fly, to raise oneself;
77		an Egg, Feminine, womanly, Child-hood.
78		Fish, Impurity, foulness, to hinder, to prevent, to stop.
79		Crocodile, Impudence, insolence, robbery, depredator, to hide.
80		Serpent, snake, reptile.
81		Sacred, snake, goddess.
82		Tree, beam, bar.
83		Wood, timber, wooden object.
84		a flower, plant, vegetable.
85		Flower, joy, pleasure, comfort.
86		Sweetness, pleasant, acceptable.
87		Season, year, 12 month, to drive, to turn, to renew.
88		Field, plain.
89		Grain, Rye, Corn, Value (coins) Harvest, crops, livelihood, custom, maintenance
90		Grain, measures, harvest, crop, tribute, bushel, weight.
91		Heaven, cover, vail, height, altitude, superiority.
92		Night, evening, eve, west, darkness, gloom.
93		Rain, shower, cloud, thunderstorm, dangle, light ring, lustre, brightness.
94		Sun, light, parts of the time.
95		Light, lustre, brightness
96		The moon & its phases.
97		star, planet, constellation, god
98		mountain, mountainous land.
99		Land, ground, people, nation
100		Island, Isle, coast, shore, sea shore.

No.	Zeichen	determiniert	No.	Zeichen	determiniert
101		Name, district, territory, field, hiss, planted with the vine.	124		To wrap up, to veil, to embalm, to reckon, count, disease, sickness.
102		Town, city, place, region	125		Smell, odour, to wind out, to sack, to bag.
103		Stone, rock, brick, to build with bricks.	126		To write, to read, to lecture, book, science, knowledge, to surround, to bind, to tie, to shut, to lock, to end, to finish
104		Ore, metal, brass, iron, made metal			
105		Water, fluidity, fluid, liquor river, mixing, to wash, purity.	127		Jewel, treasure, ring. to seal, to confirm, to shut, to lock.
106		Water, fluid, to pour out, to empty, to break open, to vomit.	128		Field, district, territory.
107		Water, pond, fluid, basin, reservoir, sea, river, flowing, wet, moisten, to overflow.	129		To cross, to crucify, to mix, to mingle, increase.
			130		Name, king's name, circle, sphere.
108		Weight, heaviness.	131		To divide, part, to separate, to part, half, middle.
			132		Seat, chair, stool.
109		House, household, room, habitation.	133		Metal, brazen, sand, powder, flower, flour, meal, resin, rosin.
110		Wall, enclosing, enclosure, fortress, fort.	134		To die, wickedness, malice, misfortune.
111		To turn, to tilt over, to break down, to break, to shatter in.	135		Heart, breast, middle, midst.
112		Staircase, stairs, to rise, mount.	136		Writing, letters, book, plan drawing, draught, design, calculation, knowing, knowledge, thought, idea, abstract idea.
113		Name, Name of a fortress, or foreign monarch.			
114		Corner, angle, nook, protection, defence.	137		Coffin, embalming.
115		Obelisk.	138		Bread, nourishment. food, quantity,
116		Pyramid, grave, tomb, great tomb, great house, heap, or hoard.	139		Breadth, latitude, to distribute.
117		Rest, repose, death, mummy, to embalm, disease, sickness.	140		Fire, to burn, heat, ardour
118		Sabre, sword, knife, cutter, slayer, to strike, to offer, sacrifice, to cut off, to separate, to write, record.	141		Festival, joy, pleasure, content, gratify
			142		Oil, fragrancy, flavour.
119		To land, disembark, foreign, foreign nation.	143		Oil, fragrancy, flavour, fluid, humour.
120		Compartment, shadow, shade.	144		To break. Roads. to break open. to break up. To depart, to separate, far, far off.
121		Chisel, to chisel, to smooth, to polish, nail, bone, ivory.	145		Ship, vessel, to travel, journey, to row, to walk.
			146		Sail, wind, air, breath, puff, vent, breeze.
122		To plough, to till the ground, to build upon, to cultivate.	147		To dress, clothe, to wrap up, to veil, to adorn, to attire.
123		To bind, to tie, to fasten, attack, to dress, clothe, to wrap up, to veil, garment, to approach.			

P.T.O.

Additional Hieroglyphics

Sep.

= Atb

Shenu, or Khenu

Sem

Ah

Set

Druck von Breitkopf und Härtel in Leipzig.

= water . . .

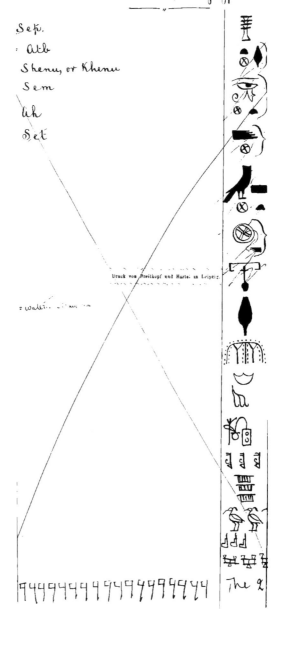

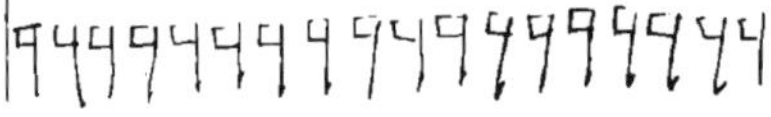

The 2

Additional Hieroglyphics.

Determinatives.

Sign of Royalty		Body		Soles of feet. sandals
Childhood		Stomach		Leg
Chief		Eye inverted		Halter
Elder		Lips		Year
Prince		Tongue		Lip
Ruler		Tooth		Sky rising.
Fall		Beard		Radiancy
Lower Egypt		Breast		Moon
Priestess		Flesh		Radiant Disk
Pure		Bone		Land
Tadpole		Fat		Land

Foundation		Complete		= 834
A kind of Cake		Black		
Cycle		Net, Snare		= 220
Land		Adze		= 3244
Canopy		East		Tillage
Embalmed		West		
House		Vessels full		= 760
Loaf of bread		" empty		= 974
Tie of linen		Great		
Papyrus		Arrow		= Life
Thicket of Papyrus		= Herb		Goodness
Wood, cut		Javelin		Goodness
Seed		Earth		Power or Purity
Place				Majesty & Dominion
Hill country		Goldsmith		Authority
Thebes				Royalty
Papyrus		Gold		"

23166319R00020

Printed in Great Britain
by Amazon